I0532434

KILLER GOD:
Is God a genocidal
mass murderer?

KERBY RIALS

© 2023 Kerby Rials

Kerby Rials

KILLER GOD: Is God a genocidal mass murderer?

All rights reserved. No part of this publication may be reproduced, stored in a retrieval system or transmited in any form or by any means, electronic, mechanical, photocopying, recording or otherwise without the prior permision of the publisher or in accordance with the provisions of the Copyright, Designs and Patents Act 1988 or under the terms of any licence permitting limited copying issued by the Copyright Licensing Angency.

ISBN-13: 979-8-9857499-9-1

Published by:
Abundance Books, LLC
417 Forest Street #445
Kalamazoo MI 49001
abundance-books.com

Distributed by:
Looking Glass River Publishing
418 Strathmore Rd.
Lansing MI 48910
TEL: 517 708 9166
EMAIL: kerbyrials@aol.com

Dedicated to Rev. Bill Bowen, Ph.D., who directed me as a young Christian to the great intellects of Christianity, so that I was never in doubt of the truth.

Special thanks to the following persons who helped in the editing of this book: Dr. Brian Lidbeck, Dr. Lori O'Dea, Dr. Thomas Wespetal, Douglas Sharp, Dr. Robert McKay, Rev. Jim Olah, Dr. Donovan Barron, David Hamilton, Rev. Glenn Branham, Rev. Steve Miller, Teresa Janzen, Sheila Rials and Pam Bebee.

GRAPHICS (in order)
1) Christ cleansing the Temple (Bernardino Mei, 1655, Public domain)
2) Noah's Ark and the Deluge (Philip Medhurst). Wikipedia Commons. File:The_Phillip_Medhurst_Picture_Torah_53._Noah%27s_Ark_and_the_Deluge._Genesis_cap_7_v_12._Hoet.jpg
3) Molech (Charles Foster, 1897, Public domain)
4) David und Goliath (Osmar Schindler, c. 1888. Public domain)
5) Selection on the ramp at Auschwitz (1944. Public domain).

All Bible quotations are from the NASB unless otherwise noted (*New American Standard Bible*. 1995, 2020. LaHabra, CA: The Lockman Foundation.)

Table of Contents

1. The genocidal God

Is God a monster?

Did he really order the killing of thousands of young children, the elderly, teenagers, infants, women and men?

That is what we read in the Bible.

Skeptics love these passages. It makes their point. The great Mark Twain called God "insane."

In a book he ordered to be published only after his death, he said God "is totally without mercy — he who is called the Fountain of Mercy. He slays, slays, slays! All the men, all the beasts, all the boys, all the babies; also all the women and all the girls. ... He makes no distinction between innocent and guilty." [1]

Top atheist Richard Dawkins went further, saying God is an "unforgiving control-freak; a vindictive, bloodthirsty ethnic cleanser, a misogynistic, homophobic, racist, infanticidal, genocidal, filicidal, pestilential, megalomaniacal, sadomasochistic, capriciously malevolent bully." [2]

Dawkins sure seems angry at someone he says does not exist! But I digress.

Because of these difficult passages, some Christians

---

1   Mark Twain, *Letters from the Earth*, Letter 11.
2   Richard Dawkins, *The God Delusion* (Mariner: Boston, 2006) p. 51

have abandoned their faith in God. How can God be good and at the same time order the deaths of millions?

These passages ARE difficult. It is very hard to reconcile them with the love of Jesus, who cared for children, fed the hungry, healed the sick and forgave. It is hard to figure out. Is God harsh, or loving? Kind or cruel? Does the Bible contradict itself?

Reading these passages leaves us three options:

1) God is a monster.

2) The Bible is wrong. Or,

3) There must be some other explanation.

This book is about option 3.

There is a better explanation, which includes the most ancient prophecy of the Bible, a test of our true intentions, the supernatural world, the Messiah, and hidden assumptions. The latter is the subject of the next chapter.

2. Check your assumptions at the door

Years ago my wife and I were invited to hear a friend sing at a shady bar. When we got there they wouldn't let us in unless we checked our coats. We felt uncomfortable with the whole trashy place, so we left.

In the same way, we can't get past the door to understand these difficult passages unless we check some assumptions at the door. It may be only temporary, but we need to leave some assumptions behind — assumptions we may not even realize we have. Otherwise it will be practically impossible to clarify these passages. There are at least five of them:

1) We have an anti-supernatural bias.

Anything that involves heaven, angels, demons or eternity is rejected out of hand by many today. It is not even considered. This despite the fact that even famous atheists like Madalyn Murray O'Hair went to séances and believed in the supernatural. (She was the atheist leader who sued successfully to ban prayer in schools.) Madalyn's son writes:

"It was during one of these séances that my mother

convinced herself that she was in direct communication with Bill Moore, the postman who had been her companion in Baltimore....Mother never tried to reconcile her atheism with conversations with dead people. After her father's death she had gone to the graveyard almost daily to talk to him. Once she sat for hours next to his grave in the rain." [3]

Mark Twain had many harsh things to say about God and the Bible late in life. He especially became embittered after the death of his daughter and wife. His personal assistant, who wrote his biography, referred to a dream Twain had which precisely predicted his little brother's death, who was soon to sail with him on a steamboat down the Mississippi. He knew, therefore, that the spiritual world exists.

"One night, … he slept at his sister's house and had this vivid dream: He saw [his brother] Henry, a corpse, lying in a metallic burial case in the sitting-room, supported on two chairs. On his breast lay a bouquet of flowers, white, with a single crimson bloom in the center. ... He told Pamela the dream, then put it out of his mind as quickly as he could. The *Pennsylvania* sailed from St. Louis as usual, and made a safe trip to New Orleans. [On its return, the ship blew up, and Henry was severely injured.] He died before morning. ... The ladies of Memphis ... bought for him a metallic [coffin]. [Twain] entering, saw his brother lying exactly as he had seen him in his dream, lacking only the bouquet. ... At that moment an elderly lady came in with a large white bouquet, and in the center of it was a single red rose." [4]

---

3   Murray, William J., *My Life Without God*, chapter 10, WND Books, Washington DC, 2012, ISBN 978-1-936488-34-6
4   Paine, Albert Bigelow, *Mark Twain, A Biography, 1835-1910, Complete: The Personal And Literary Life Of Samuel Langhorne Clemens.* Chapters XXV and XXVI.

It's not just O'Hair and Twain who believe in the supernatural — research shows that most atheists do also.

I know that sounds illogical, because it is. But here are the facts as reported by *New Scientist*:

"The UK-based Understanding Unbelief project interviewed thousands of self-identified atheists and agnostics from six countries — Brazil, China, Denmark, Japan, US and UK. It found that ...a majority believe in at least one supernatural phenomenon or entity...71 per cent of atheists hold one or more such beliefs [reincarnation or life after death]; for agnostics the figure is 92 percent." [5]

Accordingly, it's not logical to reject the supernatural reasons for the violence in the Bible. Most atheists believe in the supernatural. And, including the supernatural in our consideration of the violence in the Bible is good science, as strange as that may sound.

For example, a true scientist would never begin research vowing to reject certain conclusions beforehand. Instead he or she would let the evidence determine the conclusion.

Accordingly, rejecting the supernatural world from the outset is bad science. It is like a scientist researching the answer to 2 plus 2, who decides from the beginning that he will never accept 4 as an answer.

That is not very scientific.

And yet that is where many find themselves when pondering God's violence in the Bible. They reject any answer that involves the supernatural.

Often people try to use natural explanations for supernatural phenomena. For instance, many have offered human

---

5   https://www.newscientist.com/article/2204958-most-atheists-believe-in-the-supernatural-despite-trusting-science/, accessed Jan. 2, 2023

explanations for Jesus' resurrection. They say he didn't die — he just fainted. Some Muslims say it wasn't really Jesus who was crucified — it was someone who looked like him. Others say the apostles stole his body.

Using natural explanations for the supernatural is rejected by the Bible: "The natural person does not accept the things of the Spirit of God, for they are folly to him, and he is not able to understand them because they are spiritually discerned" (1 Cor. 2:14).

Accordingly, to understand the problem of the violence of God, we need to discern it spiritually — not from a human perspective, but from a supernatural perspective.

Let me add that "understanding from a supernatural perspective" does not mean sacrificing our intellect or believing something just because we are told to believe. Instead, it means simply being open to the reality of the spiritual world, based on objective facts and evidence.

2) We don't trust God.

Another barrier to understanding biblical violence is that we come to the subject of God with a negative viewpoint. He is already a monster in our eyes. Thus our investigation is tainted and goes astray from the beginning. It becomes a self-fulfilling prophecy. In other words, if we begin by assuming that God is evil, we will find it to be so. If we begin by assuming that God is good, we will find evidence to support that. This is called confirmation bias. We look for evidence to confirm what we already think.

For example, years ago, my dad was a supervisor for Shell Oil. He told me that occasionally when he asked a worker to do a certain job the worker would say the proce-

11

dure could not be done — that it was impossible. He said over the years, he discovered that such workers would try, but that they would always fail. They wanted to show him that it would not work. So he learned to seek out another worker, with a positive attitude to do the very same job, and that worker succeeded. Whatever the worker said, would come true. It was a self-fulfilling prophecy.

In the same way, skeptics like Richard Dawkins think God is a monster. It doesn't seem possible for them to consider God impartially. Others, like Twain, are mad at God for something. Some think God is cruel and are afraid of him. Jesus refers to such a man in Luke 19:21 who said, "I was afraid of you."

For those with such convictions, it is natural to assume the divine violence in the Bible occurred because God is evil. Those with such convictions will find it hard to believe that God's actions are justified. They will have trouble finding the truth.

3) We believe all violence is wrong.

Some cannot accept that God can be violent. In his book *The Nonviolent God* J. Denny Weaver says Pharoah's soldiers were not drowned by God for trying to enslave the Jews, but because they were in the wrong place at the wrong time. [6] Weaver cannot conceive of a violent God.

And yet we all know policemen who can save a kitten in the morning, and shoot a criminal in the afternoon. Is the policeman evil, because he is sometimes violent? Of course

6   "It was the Egyptian commanders who ordered their troops into an untenable situation. When the water returned to its natural course, the Egyptian army was done in because they were in a place they should not have been." (p.110, Weaver, J. Denny, *The Nonviolent God*, Wm. B. Eerdmans Publishing Company, Grand Rapids MI, 2013)

Christ Cleansing the Temple (Bernardino Mei, 1655).

not. He is trained and authorized to shoot people, even though he may be kind and compassionate. In the same way, soldiers who defend their country are violent, but not bad. How, then, can we be shocked when God is violent against evil?

God is kind with the good, like the policeman with the kitten, but severe with evil, like a soldier killing a terrorist.

Rom. 11:22 says this: "Behold then the kindness and severity of God; to those who fell, severity, but to you, God's kindness, if you continue in His kindness; otherwise you also will be cut off."

And yet we struggle to understand God's violence in the Old Testament, especially when Jesus seemed to advocate non-violence. He said, "But I say to you, do not resist an evil person; but whoever slaps you on your right cheek, turn the other to him also" (Matt. 5:39). [7]

This has led some to dismiss the Old Testament as false, since it shows a violent and angry God, instead of the suffering and forgiving Christ of the New Testament. Many people equate anger with sin. How can God be angry? [8]

However, the same Jesus who told us to tolerate insults such as a slap, made a whip and hit people with it, chasing them out of the temple, while overturning tables.

"And He made a scourge of cords, and drove them all out of the temple, with the sheep and the oxen; and He poured out the coins of the money changers and overturned their tables" (John 2:15).

Just in case we might be inclined to overlook this, the Lord makes sure to include this in all four of the gospels (Matt. 21:12, Mark 11:15, Luke 19:45, John 2:15).

This same Jesus, the Bible says, will return with violence.

"And I saw heaven opened, and behold, a white horse, and He who sat on it is called Faithful and True, and in righteousness He judges and wages war....He is clothed with a robe dipped in blood, and His name is called The Word of God. [9] And the armies which are in heaven ... were following Him on white horses. From His mouth comes a sharp sword, so that with it He may strike down the nations, and He will

---

7   Jesus' comments are in the context of getting personal vengeance — "an eye for an eye." He was not promoting pacifism, but was just teaching us not to avenge ourselves for insults.

8   The Bible says we can be angry and not sin (Eph. 4:26).

9   Note that only Jesus is called the Word of God; see John 1:1

rule them with a rod of iron; and He treads the wine press of the fierce wrath of God, the Almighty. And on His robe and on His thigh He has a name written, 'King of kings, Lord of lords.' ... And I saw the beast and the kings of the earth and their armies assembled to make war against Him who sat on the horse and against His army. And the beast was seized, and with him the false prophet. ... These two were thrown alive into the lake of fire which burns with brimstone. And the rest were killed with the sword which came from the mouth of Him who sat on the horse, and all the birds were filled with their flesh" (Rev. 19:11-21).

So we see no contradiction between the God of the Old Testament and the God of the New. God is the same in both. He is violent in the Old, and violent in the New, as we have just read. He is forgiving in the Old, and forgiving in the New.

In the Old Testament we read: "For You, Lord, are good, and ready to forgive, and abundant in lovingkindness to all who call upon You" (Ps. 86:5). In the New Testament we read: "But Jesus was saying, 'Father, forgive them; for they do not know what they are doing'" (Luke 23:34).

4) We are looking for an excuse.

This may sound judgmental, but it is not meant to be. Please let me explain.

Years ago I worked in an office, and had shared my faith with my boss. He was not the least interested, but had no answer against the truth of God's word.

But the day came when Jimmy Swaggart, the famous televangelist, tearfully confessed his sin with a prostitute. It was on the front page of every newspaper, and topped every news broadcast. The next day my boss was as happy as I had ever seen him! He was smiling from ear to ear, and making jokes about Jimmy's fall, which comforted him. He was looking for an excuse to justify his own sins, and Jimmy had given it to him.

In the same way some people are fixated on the violence in the Bible as they believe that gives them justification to reject God.

This was exactly the case with a man I met in Lviv, Ukraine, a month after the war started. My Jewish evangelist friend Nazar Spodar and I were sharing the gospel at the train station. One man said he was shocked at the violence of God in the Old Testament and was studying it. In fact, he said he was studying only that — nothing in the New Testament — nothing about the Jesus who was beaten, crucified and resurrected for our forgiveness.

I told him I was studying that very subject and would be happy to hear his concerns, and respond to them.

To my surprise he did not want any explanation. I did not understand, and persisted by saying he could write me an email later with any questions. But he did not want my email address either. He did not want ANY explanations. Suddenly I realized that he was studying these difficult passages not to get understanding, but to get ammunition. He was seeking an excuse to reject God and the Bible, and these passages served him well.

5) We don't believe God has the right to judge us.

We think he has no right to act. We treat God as if he were a man, instead of our creator. We judge and condemn HIM, but do not think he has the right to judge US. We judge God over things we do not understand. In Job 40:2-8 the Lord says this: "Will the faultfinder contend with the Almighty? Let him who reproves God answer... Will you condemn Me that you may be justified?" (For more on this see the chapter: *Judging God*.)

In conclusion, the five assumptions that will prevent us from finding the truth are:

1) The supernatural world does not exist.

2) God cannot be trusted.

3) God cannot be violent.

4) I don't want to believe the truth.

5) God has no right to judge us.

For the sake of argument, I suggest we set aside these assumptions for the moment.

This will help as we look at the time when God killed almost the whole world.

3. The genocidal flood

About 4,000 years ago, God killed everybody, except for eight people. This is what the Bible says, and it is supported by science (see below) and by histories preserved in every continent and in many languages.[10]

It really happened.

If ever God could be called genocidal, this would be it. This makes the Canaanites' deaths centuries later seem like

---

10   McDowell, Josh, *The New Evidence That Demands a Verdict* (Thomas Nelson Publishers, 1999), p. 104.

nothing. Why did this happen? The Bible says:

"When the Lord God saw the extent of human wicked-ness, and that the trend and direction of men's lives were only towards evil, he was sorry he had made them. It broke his heart. And he said, 'I will blot out from the face of the earth all mankind that I created. Yes, and the animals too, and the reptiles and the birds. For I am sorry I made them'" (Gen. 6:5-7 TLB).

Here we see why. People were violent, evil and demonic (more on that later). But it is still hard to accept. Men, wom-en, the elderly, children and infants all died. Even animals were killed. Only those on the ark survived.

The first inclination is to think that it did not happen — that this is a myth or a fairy tale. But geology and theology agree that the flood in the Bible is more than a story.

For instance, geology teaches us that the oil and gas that we use comes from massive amounts of plants and animals that were buried under flood sediment. Crude oil is com-posed primarily of salty sea water with only part being oil. It is a silent witness that the salty oceans did cover the world. The Bible is true. Fossils of sea creatures are even found on Mount Everest, the highest mountain in the world. [11]

Dinosaur fossils prove the flood, as only that could have preserved such huge creatures by instantly burying them in mud. Even dinosaur eggs were preserved worldwide, evidence that the flood was not local.[12] Of course, eggs are

---

11   This is not to say Everest was a mountain during the flood; it was a sea floor pushed up by the collision of the Indian subcontinent with Asia. The point here is that the earth has changed greatly since the flood. We do not know how high the mountains were at that time, since Everest was part of the sea. We only know that the Bible says all mountains were covered by flood waters: "The water prevailed more and more upon the earth, so that all the high mountains everywhere under the heavens were covered. The water prevailed fifteen cubits higher, and the mountains were covered" (Gen. 7:19-20).

12   https://www.amnh.org/dinosaurs/dinosaur-eggs, accessed May 24, 2023.

fragile and predators love to eat them. It is hard to imagine how they could be fossilized. Mudslides caused by the flood, however, would easily preserve them. The American Museum of Natural History reports: "One remarkable find was in Montana, where fossils of duckbill dinosaurs, including eggs, nests, hatchlings, juveniles, and adults were found together in one death assemblage, or mass grave." [13]

Mitochondrial DNA also proves the truth of the flood and the Bible. (This special DNA is found only in women, and changes slightly with each generation.) [14]

By studying it, scientists discovered that all women are descended from one woman (Eve), just like the Bible says. Subsequent studies of the Y-chromosome (which only males have) proved that all men are descended from one man (Adam), just like the Bible says.

These special types of DNA, amazingly, prove the biblical flood occurred. The genetic evidence says that the man from whom we are all descended lived hundreds of years later than Eve. This would make the biblical account of Adam and Eve false. They could never have met. However, this dilemma is resolved when we realize that all men are descended — not just from Adam — but also from his descendant Noah, who did live hundreds of years later. Therefore, genetics and the Bible agree. There was a flood.

Population growth rates, when applied to today's population retroactively, reveal that human population was in the single digits 5,300 years ago, just like the Bible says of the

---

13   Ibid.
14   This is from a secular website and confirms that one woman (Eve) was the ancestor of all humans, but it uses a different time line. Space does not allow comparisons of dating methodology. https://www.sciencedaily.com/releases/2010/08/100817122405.htm, accessed May 25, 2023.

eight people on the ark. [15]

The Bible is right. Even Jesus said that there was a flood.

"As it was in the time of Noah so shall it be in the days of the Son of Man. Everybody kept on eating and drinking, and men and women married, up to the very day Noah went into the boat and the flood came and killed them all" (Luke 17:26-27 GNB). So there was a flood, ordered by God, and millions of people died in it. Does that make God, then, a genocidal mass murderer?

The word genocidal has connotations of racism.

However, the Bible says God created all races, and says that people from all races and languages will be in heaven (Rev. 5:9). So God is not genocidal in terms of racism.

But if genocidal is defined as the destruction of a specific ethnic group for its wickedness, then God can be called genocidal. He ordered Israel to wipe out the Amalekites for their betrayal in attacking the Jews (who were their distant cousins) and for their godlessness:

"Remember what Amalek did to you along the way when you came out from Egypt, how he met you along the way and attacked among you all the stragglers at your rear when you were faint and weary; and he did not fear God. Therefore it shall come about when the Lord your God has given you rest from all your surrounding enemies, in the land which the Lord your God gives you as an inheritance to possess, you shall blot out the memory of Amalek from under heaven; you must not forget" (Deut. 25:17-19).

Amalek was indeed wiped out (1 Chr. 4:43).

There are none left today.

---

15   John C. Whitcomb, Jr., and Henry M. Morris, *The Genesis Flood* (Baker Book House, 1961), p. 398.

Perhaps some could also blame God for all the deaths on earth. Today as you read this millions are dying. One day you will as well.

Death was never God's plan, however. Only when we turned from God, did death begin as a natural consequence of our rebellion. "When sin has conceived, it brings forth death" (James 1:15). Further the Bible says death will be destroyed in the future: "The last enemy that will be abolished is death" (1 Cor. 15:26).

As to murder, God does not murder anyone. Murder implies unlawful death. When a criminal is put to death by the justice system, it is not murder — it is justice.

So God is not a mass murderer. He did put millions to death during the flood, but in his wisdom turned that death from a dead end (pun intended) to a gateway to eternal life. As Jesus said, "I am the resurrection and the life; he who believes in Me will live even if he dies." (John 11:25). God is not a mass murderer, but a mass life giver.

In order to preserve the way to eternal life, he had to act against the corruption in humanity which threatened the birth of the Messiah (Jesus) as is shown later in this book. Further, the evil in humanity before the flood demanded God's attention. He is obligated by his very goodness to act against evil. A superficial understanding of these two issues can lead us to judge God, which is the subject of the next chapter.

4. Judging God

Years ago my wife took our young son Luke to the doctor to get a vaccination. The doctor asked Sheila to hold Luke down while he gave him the shot.

When the pain was over, Luke sat up, looked at his mother angrily and hit her. In his toddler brain, he had 1) put her on trial as an accessory to child abuse, 2) found her guilty, 3) sentenced her to be hit, and 4) he carried out the punishment himself. He was judge, jury and executioner. No explanation of vaccination would have helped.

It is a funny story, but you and I are in the same position. We are children, and God is our parent.

We often do not understand what God is doing, and we judge him just like children judge their parents. We do not think he has the right to do what he wishes with his creation. We have even accused God of being a criminal — a mass murderer. We have trouble accepting God as our superior, and we judge God as if he were a man. However, God is not a man, any more than a parent is a child. Young children cannot judge their parents. Parents know things that their children do not. A child does not know enough to judge or condemn his parents. We do not have the capacity to judge God either. We do not know enough. He is God, and we are not, as Lester Sumrall liked to say. There is a fundamental difference between the creator and his creation, between God and humanity. Parents are not children, and God is not a man. The same rules do not apply. Once we realize that, it makes this less of a problem.

For instance, *Saturday Night Live*'s Gilda Radner once did a skit where she ranted in a TV editorial about people opposed to violins on television. She was very upset, and thought violins should be on TV! The announcer then gently explained to her that it was not VIOLINS that people were opposed to, but VIOLENCE. She smiled, and said, "Never mind!" [16] Many of us will one day say, "Never mind!" to God after ranting about violence in the Bible. We don't know everything. We misunderstand what we do know. And we have drawn wrong conclusions. Proverbs 25:8 says, "Do not go out hastily to argue your case. Otherwise, what will you do in the end, when your neighbor humiliates you?" In the same way, we should not be too hasty in accusing God of being a criminal, when he is far from that. But at the same time, we should not just shrug our shoulders and dismiss this problem. We need some kind of an answer: why would God kill all the people? All the children? All the animals? And not just once, in the flood, but in Canaan, in Sodom, and at the end of the world? The next chapter explains God's point of view.

---

16   https://www.youtube.com/watch?v=fZLeaSWY37I, accessed Dec. 28, 2022, accessed Dec. 27, 2022

5. The ancient prophecy

Why kill almost everyone on the planet with a flood? Surely they were not THAT bad? Couldn't the children have been spared?

Understanding why the flood happened is also central to understanding the destruction of the Canaanites, the Midianites, and Sodom and Gomorrah. They are parallel situations.

Each is based on mercy and justice, and not cruelty. This may seem crazy, but there is an explanation found in Gen. 3:15, which is the most ancient prophecy in the Bible. There the Lord pronounces judgment against Satan, who spoke through the serpent to deceive Eve. (Yes, there was an Eve. Remember that mitochondrial DNA research in the chapter on the flood.)

"And I will put enmity between you [Satan] and the woman, and between your seed and her seed. He shall bruise you on the head, and you shall bruise him on the heel."

Note that the prophecy referring to Eve's descendant (her seed) is grammatically singular and masculine ("he shall").

In other words, it is a promise not to all her children, but to one specific male descendant of Eve who will crush Satan. This is a prophecy of the Messiah, Jesus. Satan will hurt him ("bruise him on the heel"), which he did when Jesus was crucified and had his heels pierced with the nails. But Jesus will crush him. He will triumph over him by his resurrection, and will cast him into the lake of fire upon his return, as the Bible says in Rev. 20:10.

This is God's answer to our sin problem, and he promises it right at the beginning of the Bible. God is more concerned with our eternal fate than anything else. He is like a parent concerned with the future of his child. He wants the child to be healthy and wants him to eat vegetables. The child wants to eat candy and isn't concerned about his future at all. In the same way, God would rather we have temporary sufferings and eternal joy, instead of temporary joy and eternal suffering.

For instance, God could have put to death all of mankind at the flood, and started over. Why didn't he?

Because he had already promised to save us. He prophesied that he would save us through the Messiah, who had to be a descendant of Eve ("her seed," Gen. 3:15). The Messiah is God's only way of saving us. Jesus said, "I am the way, the truth and the life. No one comes to the Father but by me" (John 14:6).

God promised it. He cannot lie or fail to keep his word.

If all mankind is destroyed, then no descendant of Eve can be raised up to redeem us. Total annihilation means no Messiah. (Hold that thought.)

6. 75 years of preaching

God's mercy and patience are shown in the fact that it took about 75 years to build the ark. This delay in God's judgment on Noah's time was intentional. [17]

God could have executed his judgment instantly, while protecting Noah and his family. Or he could have provided the boat so Noah did not have to build it. But he told Noah to build it, and it took a long time. The ark was a huge ship, estimated at 1,322 tons empty, and one and a half football fields in length (144 meters). [18]

Like all ships, it was built on dry ground. It was probably far from the ocean. There was no need to be close, as the ocean would come to it, not the other way around.

Building such a large ship for almost a century, too big to be moved to the sea, would surely have become a subject of much interest. It is reasonable to assume that people would have come from miles around to see this huge ship. It likely became a tourist attraction: "Come see the crazy family building a ship too big to get it to the ocean!"

17   https://answersingenesis.org/bible-timeline/how-long-did-it-take-for-noah-to-build-the-ark/, accessed Dec. 5, 2022.
18   https://www.smithsonianmag.com/science-nature/could-noahs-ark-float-theory-yes-180950385/#:~:text=This%20means%20that%2C%20by%20their,a%20very%20small%20cargo%20ship, accessed Dec. 5, 2022

This lengthy construction was, I believe, part of the mercy of God. This long time gave everyone time to consider Noah's message. And Noah had a message. The Bible says he was a preacher.

"And did not spare the ancient world, but preserved Noah, a preacher of righteousness, with seven others, when He brought a flood upon the world of the ungodly" (2 Peter 2:5).

So we see God's hidden mercy here. He created a sign to get people's attention (the ark), and then he put his man, a preacher, in the middle of that, warning this violent generation for 75 years. As it says, "God is not willing that any should perish, but that all should come to repentance" (2 Peter 3:9).

God was not in a hurry to bring his judgment on the evil of that world. He gave them time to consider and to turn away — to repent. This is just what he said about Jezebel in Rev. 2:21: "I gave her time to repent."

God gives us time also, because of his love for us.

7. Even the kids?

Understanding the deaths of children is difficult.

There are many theories.

Often it is noted that God acts corporately against cultures and nations. Not all in those nations are guilty, but all suffer together.

For instance, in World War II the United States dropped nuclear bombs on Hiroshima and Nagasaki. Many innocent children died. But the bombings ended the war, saving millions of lives which would have been lost in an invasion.

It was a corporate judgment against Japan, which had caused much suffering in Asia.

Similarly, the Bible teaches that we are all children of Adam, and so we suffer from his sin due to "corporate personality." But for the same reason, we also all can benefit from Christ's sacrifice.

Theologian Dr. Thomas Wespetal quotes Rom. 5:17-18 (GNB) as an example of the dual aspect of this principle: "It is true that through the sin of one man death began to rule because of that one man. But how much greater is the result of what was done by the one man, Jesus Christ! All who receive God's abundant grace and are freely put right with him will rule in life through Christ. So then, as the one sin condemned all people, in the same way the one righteous act sets all people free and gives them life." [19]

In the Bible we see God's corporate judgment against those who lived before the flood, and of Canaan, Amalek, Midian, Sodom and Gomorrah: men, women and children. Also when God poured out judgments against other nations (like Egypt and Assyria), their children suffered as well.

These judgments begin to be more understandable when we realize that children go to heaven automatically, and that all of us must die anyway.

Another possible explanation of these judgments is that children, through no fault of their own, were spiritually compromised by the evil cultures in which they lived.

Evidence for this theory is seen in the fact that God ordered the deaths of all men, women and children in Canaan, but outside of Canaan the children were spared (see the chapter: *Fair judgment* for more on this.)

Similarly, the animals were ordered to be killed in Canaan, but they were spared outside of Canaan.

It seems logical to conclude that things were so bad in Canaan, that it even affected children and animals (See the chapter: *How bad was Canaan?*)

Could this have been because even the children and animals were demonically possessed? It is possible. In Matt. 17:18 we see Jesus casting a demon out of a child: "And Jesus rebuked the demon, and it came out of him, and the boy was healed instantly." We see a similar case in Mark 7:24-26: "Jesus got up and went away from there to the region

19   Wespetal, Thomas, *Союз с Христом*, chapter 5, https://www.russiantheologicalre-sources.com/union.html, accessed June 14, 2023.

of Tyre. ...But after hearing of Him, a woman whose little daughter had an unclean spirit immediately came and fell at His feet. Now the woman was a Gentile, of the Syrophoenician race. And she kept asking Him to cast the demon out of her daughter."

In a culture that cultivates the demonic, like the Canaanite, many children can have demons.

Does that mean that they are guilty for that? No.

For example, when a friend of mine was 10 her parents began having séances. They tried to contact dead relatives and others. She told us that her parents learned that spirits can more easily speak through children than through an adult. So they began to use her — their own daughter — as the medium for these séances.

To them it was harmless, but it harmed her.

Through no fault of her own, this young girl became demonized. The spirit she welcomed did not leave after the séance, and for the next 20 years she carried this evil within her. There was a darkness in her life that nothing could fix.

I was present with her husband for her deliverance. Our pastor commanded the spirit to leave, and it did. She screamed and her face contorted. It was absolutely real. I had never seen anything like it. The hair stood up on the back of my neck.

She was not guilty for her situation, and neither were the Canaanite children, who went straight to heaven when they died, just like those who perished in the flood in Noah's day, and just like David's son who was born of an adulterous relationship. David said that he would see his son in heaven, so this child was innocent before God (2 Sam. 12:23).

The Bible also shows animals as demon-possessed:

"When Jesus had stepped out of the boat, immediately there met him out of the tombs a man with an unclean spirit. ... And crying out with a loud voice, he said, 'What have you to do with me, Jesus, Son of the Most High God? I adjure you by God, do not torment me.' ... And Jesus asked him, 'What is your name?' He replied, 'My name is Legion, for we are many….and they begged him, saying, 'Send us to the pigs; let us enter them.' So he gave them permission. And the unclean spirits came out and entered the pigs; and the herd, numbering about two thousand, rushed down the steep bank into the sea and drowned in the sea'" (Mark 5:2-13). In the same way in Genesis 3, we see Satan possessing a snake and speaking through him. (See Rev. 12:9, 20:9, Isa. 27:1.)

The Canaanites even had sex with animals. Note that the Bible orders the death of the animal in all such cases, just as we see in the war against the Canaanites. Leviticus 20:15-16 says, "If a man has sexual relations with an animal, he must be put to death, and you must kill the animal. If a woman approaches an animal to have sexual relations with it, kill both the woman and the animal."

Deut. 27:21 says, "Cursed is the man who has sexual relations with any animal." (See also Exodus 22:19 and Lev. 18:23.)

In giving these commands, the Lord noted that the Canaanites had done all these things, so there is no doubt that they had sex with animals: Lev. 18:24 says, "Do not defile yourselves by any of these things, for by all these the nations which I am casting out before you have become defiled."

It is also important to keep in mind when considering the death of children, that God has a different view of death than we do. For those who live just for this life, there is nothing worse than death. If someone believes that there is nothing after death, then any joy we are ever to get must come in this short life. Anything that interferes with that, therefore, is unthinkable and horrific. Any suffering in life, for such people, is inexcusable. But for the Lord, there are worse things than death. For God, death is just a passageway to another life.

For example, in C.S. Lewis' last book of the *Chronicles of Narnia* series, the heroes of his seven books are all killed! What a shock to young readers!

And yet the story does not end there. He continues to write as they pass from this world into the glories of the next. This illustrates God's point of view. This life is not the end. It's just a bump in the road. The joy of heaven awaits us, and the sufferings of this life will be forgotten.

Notice what the Bible says:

For, behold, I create new heavens and a new earth: and the former shall not be remembered, nor come into mind (Isaiah 65:17). He will wipe every tear from their eyes. There will be no more death or mourning or crying or pain, for the old order of things has passed away (Rev. 21:4).

So seeing death as the most horrible thing possible, is not God's view. For instance, many of those who died in the flood were likely in right standing with God. We would call them Christians today, even though they disobeyed in some way. They still went to heaven, as we see in Peter's remark: "For Christ ... went and made proclamation to the spirits in prison, ... who once were disobedient, when the patience of God kept waiting in the days of Noah, during the construction of the ark." (1Peter 3:18-20. See the footnote for a fuller explanation.) [20]

In the same way, the children who died in the flood automatically went to heaven after they died, because they were not conscious of good or evil and could not sin ("your children who do not yet know good from bad," Deut. 1:39. Rom. 5:13 says, "Sin is not taken into account where there is no law.") [21]

Jesus confirmed God's acceptance of children when he said, "Let the little children come to me, for of such is the Kingdom of God" (Matt. 19:14).

So here we have an answer to the deaths of these children and many of the adults who died in the flood: They are still alive in heaven. They died, but all of us will die. The only difference with those who died in the flood is that they all died at the same time.

Yet some may say that it was not fair for God to give these children short lives. We could add that it is also not fair that some children are born handicapped, and some are born into poverty. The Bible addresses all of these inequities in Rom. 9:20-21 (GNB):

"But who are you, my friend, to talk back to God? A

---

20   1 Pet. 3:18-20 and 4:6 say that "Christ ... proclaimed to the spirits in prison, because they formerly did not obey, when God's patience waited in the days of Noah, while the ark was being prepared. ... For this is why the gospel was preached even to those who are dead, that though judged in the flesh, ... they might live in the spirit." Christ did not speak to all the dead but only to the righteous. These were in the upper half of Sheol (Hades) until Christ's resurrection, as in Luke 16 with Abraham and Lazarus, comforted in paradise, and yet not seen with the Lord. See also Eph. 4:8, John 20:17, and Luke 16:26.
21   The Bible shows that young children automatically go to heaven because they are not conscious of good or evil (Deut. 1:39, Rom. 5:13). Also Is. 7:14-16 speaks of the age when a young child "knows how to refuse the evil and choose the good." Children who die before this "age of accountability" are judged as innocent by God. After that age they need to make a decision to trust Christ for forgiveness of their sins.

clay pot does not ask the man who made it, 'Why did you make me like this?' After all, the man who makes the pots has the right to use the clay as he wishes, and to make two pots from the same lump of clay, one for special occasions and the other for ordinary use."

I have a dear friend who raised a severely autistic son for 33 years. His son could not walk, and had to wear a diaper. Imagine changing the diaper of a 33-year-old man. And yet he and his wife have told me how much love they got from their son. They said he was incredibly special, and his caretakers said the same thing at his funeral. God did something special in that young man. Can we accuse God of being evil in allowing him to be born? I don't think we know enough to say that. God does indeed choose some people for a special role, that we regard as difficult, just like he did with the man born blind in John 9:1-3. The point is these cases exist only during this temporary life. They will be made right in eternity, as happened with Lazarus: "He is being comforted here...." (Luke 16:25).

It is impossible to judge these cases (of children dying young) without also including eternity. Unfortunately, those who ignore the reality of the afterlife will not be able to understand this, because they have only part of the picture.

In eternity, children will shine and never remember their sufferings (Isa. 65:17). We see their sufferings now, but something much better is to come. The apostle Paul writes in the Bible: "I consider that what we suffer at this present time cannot be compared at all with the glory that is going to be revealed to us" (Rom. 8:18 GNB).

8. How bad was Canaan?

In Genesis, God tells Abraham that his descendants would one day possess the land of Canaan (modern day Israel).

But not yet. He said they would have to wait 400 years, because the Canaanites were not yet bad enough.

This reveals a lot. Primarily it shows that God's order to the Jews to dispossess the Canaanites was because they were completely corrupted. It was eviction for cause, so to speak.

This is quite a statement. Here is the specific passage:

"In the fourth generation they will return here, for the iniquity of the Amorite [Canaanite] is not yet complete" (Gen. 15:16).

So how bad WERE the Canaanites? How complete was their wickedness?

First off, archaeological and contemporary evidence shows that the Canaanites burned children alive as a sacrifice to their god Molech, particularly in Carthage (a city in Tunisia founded and settled by Canaanites). Many Mediterranean coastal cities were founded by Canaanites (Phoenician traders) who brought with them their language, culture, religion and deities, including Molech.

"The archaeological evidence from the sacrificial precinct at Carthage thus provides striking confirmation …of child sacrifice…. It also substantiates at least indirectly, the Phoenician [Canaanite] origin of the practice." [22]

Sacrificed burned remains of hundreds of infants were found not only at Carthage but in nearby Sousse. [23]

Contemporary writers also documented this practice. Diodorus of Sicily writes: "Himilcar…supplicated the gods after the custom of his people by sacrificing a young child to Cronus" [identified with the Canaanite deity of Baal]. [24] He also writes of a second incident: "When they…saw their enemy encamped before their walls…they selected 200 of the noblest children and sacrificed them publicly…There was in their city a bronze image of Cronus, extending its hands, palms up and sloping toward the ground, so that each of the children when placed hereupon rolled down and fell into a sort of gaping pit filled with fire."

The Bible confirms the child sacrifice of the surrounding Canaanite culture.

A specific example is in 2 Kings 3:26: "When the king of Moab saw that the battle was too fierce for him, ... he took his oldest son who was to reign in his place, and offered him as a burnt offering on the wall."

The Lord warned Israel not to follow the examples of the surrounding peoples in Deut. 20:17:18:

"But you shall utterly destroy them, ... so that they may not teach you to do according to all their detestable things which they have done for their gods, so that you would sin

---

22   Mosca, Paul, doctoral thesis presented to Harvard University, Department of Near Eastern Languages and Civilizations, May 1975, p. 42.
23   ibid, p. 43
24   ibid, p. 4

Offering to Molech, Charles Foster, 1897.
against the Lord your God."

But they did not listen.

"They built the high places of Baal that are in the valley of Ben-hinnom to cause their sons and their daughters to pass through the fire to Molech, which I had not commanded them nor had it entered My mind that they should do this abomination, to cause Judah to sin" (Jer. 32:35).

Even King Solomon, the son of King David, worshipped Molech: "Then Solomon built a high place for Chemosh the detestable idol of Moab, on the mountain which is east of Jerusalem, and for Molech the detestable idol of the sons of Ammon" (1 Kings 11:7). Jewish King Ahaz also burned some of his sons alive to Molech (2 Chr. 28:3). This despite the Lord's strict command: "You shall not give any of your offspring to offer them to Molech, nor shall you profane the name of your God; I am the Lord" (Lev. 18:21).

The Bible adds more detail so that we can say that God was justified in his actions against Canaan — if we were God's judge, which we aren't.

As mentioned in the previous chapter, the Bible says the Canaanites, "the people of the land, who were before you, did all of these abominations, so that the land became unclean." (Lev. 18:27).

These abominations were:

• They had sex with animals (Lev. 18:23).

• As mentioned, they burned their children alive to their idols (Lev. 18:21).

• They practiced every type of sexual perversion known to man, including sex with their mothers, their grandchildren, and other close relatives (Lev. 18:7, 18:10).

• They were so demonic that they had relations with demons and children by them. More on this in the next chapter.

Deut. 18:10-12 also says the Canaanites burned their sons or daughters alive, practiced divination, told fortunes, and interpreted omens. They were sorcerers, charmers, mediums, necromancers and inquirers of the dead. The Lord said "whoever does these things is an abomination to the Lord. And because of these abominations the Lord your God is driving [the Canaanites] out before you."

Joshua was evidently so shocked by the evil of the Canaanites when he conquered their city of Jericho that he forbid anyone from rebuilding the city.

"Then Joshua made them take an oath at that time, saying, 'Cursed before the Lord is the man who rises up and builds this city Jericho; with the loss of his firstborn he shall lay its foundation, and with the loss of his youngest son he shall set up its gates'" (Joshua 6:26).

This was a level of corruption that no country on the earth practices today. To my knowledge there is no place today where sex with animals and burning of children alive are practiced. So we see that the Lord's judgment on these cultures was not without reason.

As bad as these things were in Canaan, in Sodom and Gomorrah, and in the pre-flood world, there was yet another level of corruption that seemed to trigger God's judgments: when women had children by demons.

This is the controversial subject of the next chapter.

9. Children of demons

More than once I have met people with crackpot conspiracy theories. I am sure you have as well. Often what they say makes me want to cringe. Often it has to do with sex.

That is why I wish I did not have to include this chapter. It has all the marks of that kind of thing. The difference here is that this one has biblical support. And it is something with which I have personal experience. It can't be dismissed, even if I wanted.

The apostle Paul said, "I did not shrink from declaring to you the whole purpose of God" (Acts 20:27). I also do not want to hide anything from you. Accordingly, let us proceed.

The Bible seems to show in two scriptures that demons have had children with women. Some accept this interpretation and some do not. However, this principle plays a role in understanding the divine violence in the Bible. That is why it is included here. The first reference is in Gen. 6:2-7 (ESV):

The sons of God saw that the daughters of men were beautiful; and they took wives for themselves, whomever they chose. Then the Lord said, "My Spirit shall not strive with man forever, because he also is flesh; nevertheless his days shall be 120 years." The Nephilim were on the earth in those days, and also afterward, when the sons of God came in to the daughters of man and they bore children to them. These were the mighty men who were of old, the men of renown. The Lord saw that the wickedness of man was great in the earth, and that every intention of the thoughts of his heart was only evil continually. And the Lord regretted that he had made man on the earth, and it grieved him to his heart. So the Lord said, "I will blot out man whom I have created from the face of the land, man and animals and creeping things and birds of the heavens, for I am sorry that I have made them."

To understand this passage first we must realize that "sons of God" usually refers to angels — both fallen ones (demons) and holy ones (angels). This is seen in three scriptures in Job, all of which refer to angels in heaven, some fallen (like Satan) and some not:

"Now there was a day when the *sons of God* came to present themselves before the Lord, and Satan also came among them" (Job 1:6).

"Again there was a day when the *sons of God* came to present themselves before the Lord, and Satan also came among them to present himself before the Lord" (Job 2:1).

"When the morning stars sang together And all the *sons of God* shouted for joy?" (Job 38:7).

Therefore most of the early Jewish and Christian writers interpreted this Genesis passage as referring to fallen angels or demons (*Nephilim*, from the word *Naphal* — fallen).

The second verse supporting this concept is found in

Jude 1:6-7. It refers to fallen angels (demons, or nephilim) "who did not keep their proper domain, but left their own habitation, ... having given themselves over to sexual immorality and gone after strange flesh." So here we see that demons can commit sexual immorality. The "strange flesh" may be a reference to women.

More than 1,600 years ago St. Augustine wrote of these demonic relations: "Many have verified it by their own experience and trustworthy persons have corroborated the experience others told, that sylvans and fauns, commonly called incubi [demons], have often made wicked assaults upon women." [25] "We have read that the fruit of the connection between those who are called angels of God and the women they loved were not men like our own breed, but giants." [26]

Demonic sexual relations with humans have been recorded worldwide for many centuries. [27]

The two biblical accounts say that demons found receptive women and literally had sex with them. Only in more recent times has this been reinterpreted by some to mean something else. I believe this is because many today have no concept of the demonic and are anti-supernatural. The possibility of demons having sex with women is dismissed as ridiculous. But is it ridiculous? First of all, the plain sense of the passages is just that. It is hard to read them any other way. [28]

---

25   https://files.romanroadsstatic.com/materials/romans/nicene-christianity/City%20 of%20God.pdf, accessed Dec. 5, 2022.

26   *The City of God*, chapter 23.

27   https://www.ancient-origins.net/myths-legends/incubi-and-succubi-crushing-night-mares-and-sex-craving-demons-part-i-006157, accessed May 30, 2023

28   Theologian William McDonald, writing in the *Believer's Bible Commentary*, notes that "Mat 22:30 is used to prove that Jesus taught that the angels don't marry. What the verse actually says, however, is that the angels in heaven neither marry nor are given in marriage. Angels appeared in human form to Abraham (Gen 18:1-5), and it seems from the text that the two who went to Sodom had human parts and emotions."

Secondly, the Bible has been proven accurate archaeologically, historically, scientifically, and prophetically. Given that, it does not seem appropriate to make an exception here. The Bible is reliable. [29]

Lastly, I got a personal confirmation of this interpretation many years ago. I was asked to help pray for an airline stewardess in Geneva, Switzerland. She had already gone through deliverance but wanted additional prayer. She had been meeting with two older women missionaries, and they had asked senior missionary Greg Fitch to help, as this was out of their league. Greg asked me to go with him.

I say this because it was evident from the time we met that she was embarrassed. Her lady friends were listening, and we were men whom she did not know. She was ashamed of what she was about to tell us.

She started by telling us she had been involved in automatic handwriting. This is when a person's hand is controlled by a demonic spirit. The spirit writes messages using the person's hand, often with different handwriting. [30]

Under questioning by Greg, she said that the demon wrote love notes, seducing her until they had actual sex. She said it was the real thing. There was an awkward silence after she said that. It was clear that she did not want to tell us, which confirmed to us that this was real. She only told us because she was desperate for help.

Now, many years after this incident, I believe the Lord wanted me to know about these things, so that I could understand what happened before the flood and in Canaan.

The Lord attacked the corruption in both cases not be-

29   McDowell, Josh, *The New Evidence that Demands a Verdict* (Thomas Nelson Publishers, 1999).
30   https://www.britannica.com/topic/automatic-writing

David and Goliath, Osmar Schindler, c. 1888.

cause he hated those people, but because the salvation of mankind was threatened. It was not because God hated Canaanites. Some Canaanites will be in heaven, and the Canaanite prostitute Rahab is even an ancestor of Jesus! (See Matt. 1:2). The command to wipe out the Canaanites, therefore, was not due to their race, but due to the demonic corruption in their cultures. As mentioned earlier, the Messiah (the seed of Eve) would crush Satan. But he had to be born first. The Messiah, as the prophet Isaiah predicted, would be God himself, born of a woman, a descendant of Eve:

"For a child will be born to us, a son will be given to us; And the government will rest on His shoulders; And His name will be called Wonderful Counselor, Mighty God, Eternal Father, Prince of Peace." (Isa. 9:6)

It is hard to imagine, therefore, that God would be born in a body that was descended from demons. This can never be. The Lord said to Israel: "You are to be holy to Me, for I the Lord am holy; and I have set you apart from the peoples to be Mine" (Lev. 20:26).

God is holy and cannot be born in a body that is half demonic and half human. This explains the command to the Israelites not to intermarry with the Canaanites. The Messiah had to be a descendant of Abraham. God told him:

"In your seed all the nations of the earth shall be blessed, because you have obeyed My voice" (Gen. 22:18).

Therefore we can understand the Lord's horror at seeing that humanity was now mixed with demons. Right after this demonic corruption, the Lord determined to wipe out 99 percent of humanity in the flood.

There are, however, arguments against this theory of demonic corruption. Some note that Jesus said that angels do not marry ("For in the resurrection they neither marry nor are given in marriage, but are like angels in heaven," Matt. 22:30). It is therefore argued that demons are incapable of having physical children.

However, this seems to contradict the plain sense of Genesis 6 and Jude 1:6-7, as mentioned.

Secondly, we should note that angels are different than demons, and marriage is different than sex. Genesis 6 and Jude 1:6-7 describe demons (not angels) having sex (not marriage). Demons are by definition disobedient to God, and they are not bound by the rules against sex or marriage that angels must obey.

Thirdly, as to whether demons can have physical children, note that angels can take physical form indistinguishable from humans, as when the two angels went to Sodom (Gen. 19). Similarly, we see that Satan can take the form of an angel. "No wonder, for even Satan disguises himself as an angel of light" (2 Cor. 11:14).

Lastly, we also see that demons and Satan's followers can do miracles, which would include, it seems, the ability to have children. Jesus said, "False Christs and false prophets will arise and will show great signs and wonders ..." (Matt. 24:24). The apostle Paul wrote that the coming of the anti-christ will be with "all power and signs and false wonders" (2 Thes. 2:9). The apostle John warns of the false prophet who will perform "great signs, so that he even makes fire come down out of heaven to the earth in the presence of men. And he deceives those who dwell on the earth because of the signs which it was given him to perform ..." (Rev. 13:13-14).

This is an area where good people can have different opinions. However, it is clear that the children born of these unions — whether from demons or not — were very unlike other humans (very big) and that God took care to wipe them out in both the flood and later in the land of Canaan (1 Sam. 17:4-5, Deut. 2:21, Gen. 14:53:11 2 Sam. 21:15-22).

This makes sense if these beings were children of demons. If they were ordinary people, as some would argue, then this would make no sense. Evidence of genetic demonic corruption in people is shown in the Bible as the birth of very large people — giants, if you want to use that term, although historical records of people of similar height exist. [31]

Note also that the *Nephilim* of Genesis 6 are the same as the giants mentioned later in the Bible (like Goliath). The same Hebrew word is used in Genesis 6 and Numbers 13:33: *Nephilim*. In Numbers it describes these Nephilim as giants. Accordingly, the "mighty men of renown" of Genesis 6 had to have also been giants: "There also we saw the Nephilim (the sons of Anak are part of the Nephilim); and we became like grasshoppers in our own sight, and so we were in their sight." Also note a peculiar phrase regarding the Nephilim giants: "The Nephilim were on the earth in those days, and also afterward" (Gen. 6:4). "And also afterward" means that giants of Genesis 6 were also born after the flood, possibly in Moses' time, since the Bible says Moses wrote Genesis. [32]

So this is additional evidence that the demonic corruption of Genesis 6 was likely repeated in Canaan. Mankind had again descended to a nadir of evil, and again God acted, in judgment against Canaan.

Lastly, just as in Genesis 6 the birth of the promised Messiah was endangered by these demonic inroads into the gene pool, here again the same threat surrounds the people from whom the Messiah must be born. This helps clarify why God ordered the extermination of the Canaanites. It was

---

31   https://www.guinnessworldrecords.com/records/hall-of-fame/robert-wadlow-tallest-man-ever, accessed July 1, 2023.

32   Theologian Victor P. Hamilton, writing in the *New International Commentary on the Old Testament,* notes that the Hebrew refers to multiple incidences; hence it can be applied to the time after the flood as well: "I understand the imperfect verb here, and in Gen 6:1, to have frequentative force. .... What is envisaged here is not one single event, but a scenario that is ongoing and habitual."

done to preserve the way of salvation for humanity, just as was done in Genesis 6.

Theologian David Guzik writes of Gen. 6:1-3: "We can deduce why Satan sent his angels to intermarry ... with human women. Satan tried to pollute the genetic 'pool' of mankind with a satanic corruption, to put a genetic 'virus' to make the human race unfit for bringing forth the Seed of the woman — the Messiah, promised in Gen. 3:15. 'If Satan could succeed in infecting the entire race, the deliverer could not come.' (Boice) And Satan almost succeeded. The race was so polluted that God found it necessary to start again with Noah and his sons…"

Was God right to remove these demonic half-breeds from humanity's gene pool?

First, as mentioned by Guzik, we see the barrier these beings caused to the birth of the Messiah. This is the principal reason God removed them, I believe. God had in mind the salvation of all mankind.

Secondly, we have a clue as to what these beings were like in the Hebrew words used to describe them: Zamzummims (plotters/intriguers), Nephilim (fallen giants), Emim (terrors), and Rephaim (giants). Such gigantic, terrifying tyrants could dominate mankind, such as Og, one of the giants, who had risen to become king of Bashan (Deut. 3:11), and Goliath, who terrified Israel. These beings were part of the genetic war waged by Satan, which is the subject of the next chapter.

10. Genetic Wars

As already seen, the Bible shows an attempt to inject a demonic genetic strain into humanity in order to prevent the birth of the Messiah.

The Bible also shows other attempts to exterminate the Jewish people, through whom the Messiah had to be born.

Pharaoh ordered all male Jewish children to be killed in Egypt (Exodus 1:8-22). A few hundred years later, the Persian King Ahasuerus ordered all Jews to be killed (Esther 3:13). King Herod ordered all the male toddlers around Bethlehem to be killed, in an attempt to stop the Messiah's birth (Matt. 2:16).

The Bible says all Jews were expelled from Rome in the first century (Acts 18:2). Jews were also expelled from England in 1290, France in 1306 and 1394, Spain in 1492 and Portugal in 1496.

The czars of Russia forced most Jews to live in poverty far from Moscow, in the Pale of Settlement, where they were beaten, raped and killed in repeated pogroms.

The Holocaust, Adolph Hitler's genocidal war against the Jewish people, is well known.

Jews have been hated and persecuted throughout history.

Recently rapper Kanye West lost more than a billion dollars in endorsements due to his anti-semitism. This hatred makes no sense. It is hard to understand why, unless the supernatural world is considered. This supernatural link reveals itself in the following situation.

In 2018 thousands of Palestinian protesters were upset that the US had recognized Jerusalem as the capital of Israel. These protests continued for a year and a half. Up to 10,000 demonstrators at a time tried to break through border defenses. Israeli forces used tear gas and then live fire to stop them. 223 Palestinian were killed. [33]

What so moved these young people to march to their deaths? Why were they so angry over something that happened 75 years ago, when Palestine was partitioned into Jordan and Israel? These young protesters had never lived in Israel. Most had never even seen it. But they were willing to die for it. Why? This question is even more puzzling when similar cases of population displacements are considered:

1) In 1945, millions of Germans were forcibly removed from Prussia, Czechoslovakia and the eastern part of Germany. Their lands were taken by the Russians, Czechs and the Poles. None of the Germans who were kicked out have been willing to die over it. Today they don't even mention it. [34]

2) About the same time the partition of India occurred. Millions were displaced as it split into Muslim and Hindu nations (Pakistan, Bangladesh and India). None of their descendants are willing to die for that today, and they are not

asking for their land back. No one is protesting anymore.[35]

3) A similar partition in the 1920s resulted in the forcible removal of two million Christian Greeks from Turkey and 600,000 Muslim Turks from Greece. They lost their homes and their jobs. But none of their descendants are willing to die for it today. They have gotten on with their lives. [36]

So why haven't the Palestinians been able to do the same? Why are they different? Why would they care if Jerusalem is recognized as Israel's capital? There is no logical reason. But there is a supernatural reason.

The return of Jerusalem to the Jews, which upset the protesters so much, was predicted by Jesus himself 2,000 years ago in Luke 21:24. Jesus said the Jewish nation would "fall by the edge of the sword and be led captive among all nations, and Jerusalem will be trampled underfoot by the Gentiles, until the times of the Gentiles are fulfilled."

His prophecy has been fulfilled to the letter. The Jews have been scattered all over the world, and the city was controlled by Gentiles (non-Jews) until 1967. This return of control opens the prophetic door to the events that must precede the return of Jesus Christ. Satan (yes he does exist) does not want this door opened, as it signals his coming end.

The Bible says, "Woe to you, O earth and sea, for the devil has come down to you in great wrath, because he knows that his time is short!" (Rev. 12:12).

So he is inspiring Palestinians and others to oppose this Jewish control of Jerusalem. This anti-Israeli attitude has continued despite the peacemaking efforts of US presidents

---

35   https://exhibits.stanford.edu/1947-partition/about/1947-partition-of-india-pakistan, accessed May 30, 2023
36   https://www.aljazeera.com/program/al-jazeera-world/2018/2/28/the-great-population-exchange-between-turkey-and-greece

Jews at the Auschwitz concentration camp, being selected for execution, May 1944.

from Nixon to Carter to Clinton to Obama to Biden, despite the UN, and despite 75 years. Time heals all wounds, but not this one. It makes no human sense, but it makes perfect sense when we see God's explanation in the Bible.

This is a continuation of the genetic wars. Jews are hated for spiritual reasons, not for human ones — not because of any evil they have done, but because they are the chosen people of God. Satan has played genetic war against this people, because salvation is from the Jews, as Jesus said in John 4:22. This desire to destroy the genetic descendants of Abraham is because there is a blessing in these people. As mentioned, God promised Abraham "through you all nations of the earth will be blessed" (Gen. 22:18).

By the same token, we see in scripture that God sets an end date on certain groups, because they are not a blessing. He determines that their genetic descendants will no longer live and multiply on his earth. This is his right as our creator, and his responsibility as a righteous judge.

These people and their descendants were at cross purposes with God's desire to save humanity.

We see this in the Amalekites also. God ordered Moses to exterminate these people, because they had attacked Israel, through whom the Messiah would be born, and they had done so without cause. This also explains the Lord's command to Moses to wipe out the Midianites, who had also tried to corrupt Israel, as we see in the next chapter.

11. Midian

Reading Numbers 31 is shocking.

Here the Bible lists exactly what happened to the Midianites, in a war God ordered: All the men, women, and boys were killed, but the young girls were spared.

Critics like Mark Twain say the girls were spared so they could be raped by Israeli men and become sex slaves. They blame God for that, and for killing the Midianites.

This is quite a charge to lay at God's feet. If it is as critics say, then God truly is a monster, or else the Bible is just a creation of evil people.

But there are answers, no matter what Mark Twain wrote.

First, the judgment on the Midianites was due to many of the same issues already discussed in this book. So there is that. But there are also additional specific answers that relate only to the Midianites:

First of all, this war was not genocide against Midian. We see the Midianites were still in huge numbers not long after the events of Numbers 31. (See Judges 6-8). They were primarily a nomadic people. So we see that this attack was only against one sub-group of Midianites who were demonically influenced to destroy Israel. More on this below. This

was not a racial war, therefore, as only some of the Midianites were affected. It was instead a spiritual war.

Second, the idea that the Jews tested each girl for virginity is not true.   Then, as now, you can quickly see who is
married and who is not. When I was in Russia, for instance, I
wore my wedding ring on my left hand, as is our custom. But
before long I discovered several Russian women seemed too
friendly, and I realized that it was because in Russia a ring on
the left hand means you are divorced and open to marriage!
(They wear their wedding rings on the right hand.)

Marital status is also clear in other cultures. In some,
married women cut their hair, or wear different clothing. For
instance, Tamar had special clothing to show her unmarried
status (2 Sam. 13:18). So there was no humiliating virginity
test as some allege.

Third, it is a mistake to see this war as anything other
than a judgment of God. It can only be understood from a
spiritual perspective. If one removes the spiritual dimension,
it is a bloody and cruel war. If one looks at it from God's
perspective, he judged a demonic culture that endangered
humanity's salvation. It threatened the nation from whom the
Messiah must come. In so acting, God was protecting humanity and showing mercy to us all — ironically, to the Midianites as well. We need a savior and they did, too. All have
sinned and fallen short of the glory of God (Rom. 3:23).

God chose to end the earthly lives of this group of Midianites for their good and ours, as hard as that is to process.
Does God have the right to end your life or my life? Yes he
does. He can do it whenever and however he chooses. Since

we are all going to die, the only difference for the Midianites was that they all died at the same time. God has eternity in mind, while we are concerned with our temporary earthly lives. When those two come into conflict, God chooses our eternal well-being over our temporary prosperity.

Fourth, the idea of sex slaves is sensational and incorrect. The Bible describes marriage here. If an Israeli desired to marry a captive, she had all the rights of a wife:

> When you go out to battle against your enemies, ... and see among the captives a beautiful woman, ... and would take her as a wife for yourself [you shall] be her husband and she shall be your wife...If you are not pleased with her, then you shall let her go wherever she wishes; but you shall certainly not sell her for money, you shall not mistreat her, because you have humbled her (Deut. 21:10-14).

The Midianite girls were by definition too young for marriage. They probably became servants in families and were treated as daughters, just as is shown in this case from the Bible of a Jewish captive in nearby Syria: "Now the Arameans had gone out in bands and had taken captive a little girl from the land of Israel, and she waited on Naaman's wife" (2 Kings 5:2-3).

Fifth, differences between males and females could explain why the boys were put to death.
• Men are more violent. They commit 96 percent of all

homicides worldwide. [37]

• Ninety percent of people in prison are male. [38]

• The male hormone testosterone makes men more prone to anger, aggression, competition, dominance and physical violence. [39]

• Also as a result of testosterone, men are 30 to 40 percent stronger than women, and are larger and heavier. [40]

• Men are leaders. Of the top Fortune 500 U.S. companies, 91 percent are led by men. Men can lead correctly, or incorrectly. They can be inspired by God, or inspired by the devil. In this case, they were inspired demonically. This was a corrupted culture. [41]

Perhaps for all these reasons the Lord determined that the males of these demonically directed cultures were more dangerous to Israel, and should be eliminated.

Sixth, the Midianites knew that what they were doing was wrong because they could see the miraculous nature of God's presence with Israel.

• The Midianites would have known that the Israelites lived off of manna that appeared each morning miraculously. The Midianite women had been with the Jewish men in close and romantic relationships, and could not have escaped knowing about this (Ex. 16:35).

---

37   https://alexaanswers.amazon.com/question/4jmjR6NLpJqqWGCBVlLt6B, accessed July 1, 2023.

38   https://www.prisonpolicy.org/women.html?gclid=Cj0KCQiAqOucBhDrARIsAPCQL1ZIw BQ-P_K34It5ElfxesIUxhAjhxy1rC7QdwlYeNGKzS-iwNrx_T4aAlPAEALw_wcB, accessed July 1, 2023.

39   https://pubmed.ncbi.nlm.nih.gov/23843821/, accessed July 1, 2023.

40   https://scholar.princeton.edu/sites/default/files/brzycki/files/mb-2002-01.pdf, accessed July 1, 2023.

41   https://www.prnewswire.com/news-releases/8-8-fortune-500-ceos-are-women---the-highest-of-all-indices--according-to-the-women-ceos-in-america-report-2022--301630455. html#:~:text=8.8%25%20Fortune%20500%20CEOs%20are,CEOs%20in%20America%20 Report%202022, accessed July 1, 2023.

• The Bible says God led Israel through a miraculous pillar of fire by night over the tabernacle, and a pillar of cloud by day. This was something the Midianites had to have heard about or seen (Ex. 13:21). The whole region had heard of how God had been with Israel, as the Canaanite Rahab said at the time: "I know that the Lord has given you the land, … for we have heard how the Lord dried up the water of the Red Sea before you when you came out of Egypt, and what you did to the two kings of the Amorites who were beyond the Jordan, to Sihon and Og, whom you utterly destroyed" (Joshua 2:9-10).

• These miracles of God had so alarmed the Midianites that they sent for Balaam to curse Israel; they correctly understood that this was a spiritual conflict, not a military one.

• The prophet that Midian and Moab hired to curse Israel, instead blessed them, and warned the Midianites and the Moabites that this was a supernaturally blessed people. This was a clear warning to them of what they were dealing with — not just anyone, but the people of God. Balaam even prophesied that the Messiah would come from Israel: "I see him, but not now; I behold him, but not near; a star shall come forth from Jacob, a scepter shall rise from Israel" (Num. 24:17).

This was really what was at stake — the Messiah. Through Balaam God warned them not to harm the Israelites, but they persisted anyway. So they were far from innocent in this affair. They had seen with their own eyes, they had heard Balaam's warnings with their ears, and undoubtedly the Holy Spirit testified to their consciences not to fight against God here, but they went ahead anyway.

Seventh, the Midianites went to great lengths to execute their strategy against Israel. It took effort and determination. They had to convince thousands of their women to seduce Jewish men. They had to transport them significant distances. They had to instruct them to bring the men to worship at their idol temples. They followed the advice of Balaam to the letter. "Behold, these [women] caused the sons of Israel, through the counsel of Balaam, to trespass against the Lord in the matter of Peor, so the plague was among the congregation" (Num. 31:16). 24,000 Jews died of this plague, which was a judgment of God (Num. 25:9).

So the strategy the Midianites used was effective. They knew what they were doing. It was a demonically inspired attack against Israel. Balaam knew that no curse would work against Israel, and so he devised a strategy to lead the Jews into the idolatry which would cause God to punish them himself.

"While Israel remained at Shittim, the people began to play the harlot with the daughters of Moab. For they invited the people to the sacrifices of their gods, and the people ate and bowed down to their gods. So ... the Lord was angry against Israel" (Num. 25:1-3).

As a result of this plot, the Lord said to Moses, "Take all the leaders of the people and execute them in broad daylight before the Lord, so that the fierce anger of the Lord may turn away from Israel. So Moses said to the judges of Israel, 'Each of you slay his men who have joined themselves to Baal of Peor'" (Num. 25:4-5).

Eighth, note that God did not hate the Midianites, as Moses' wife was a Midianite, his kids were half Midianite, and his beloved father-in-law was a priest of God and a Midianite (Exodus 3:1). Therefore, this judgment affected only a part of the Midianite peoples.

The Midianites were descended from Abraham, just as the Jews were. They were distant cousins (Gen. 25:21-22). So the accusation of genocide is simply wrong.

Again God's purpose was to preserve the only way humankind could be saved — through the Messiah. This sub-group of Midianites had already shown that they were inspired by the same demonic spirit that would later move Herod, Haman and Hitler to attack the Jews and the Messiah.

Jesus, the Messiah, is our only hope, and the Midianites were attacking that hope. Jesus said, "I am the way, the truth and the life. No one comes to the Father but by me" (John 14:6). He is the only way.

12. Fair judgment

Is God fair? Is there justice in his commands to kill the people in Canaan?

True justice takes into account the motives and knowledge of the criminal and adjusts accordingly. Not every society is equally corrupt. One size does not fit all.

The Bible says that God's judgment of us at the end of the world will be fair and vary from person to person: Luke 10:12-14, Luke 12:47-48, Luke 20:47 and James 3:1.

We see the same fairness in Canaan, although it dealt with societies.

There are six levels of judgment shown, each progressively more severe. The judgment depended not only on the corruption in the societies, but their nearness to Israel. The closer they were to Israel the more severe the judgment. In this it seems the two factors were the evil in these societies and the danger that their practices would influence Israel, from whom the Messiah was to come. Hence the judgments were both punitive and protective.

This shows that God's decision was not arbitrary, but fit the circumstances of each group.

1. The most severely judged was Jericho. It was the only city in which no one was spared, all the animals were killed and all valuable objects were destroyed except for metals, and these could not be kept but had to be given for the tabernacle. It also had the distinction of being the only city that was destroyed with an order not to rebuild it (Josh. 6:24-26).

2. The second level of judgment was for Canaan and Amalek.

For these areas, all people and animals were killed, but the Israelis could keep the valuable objects they found, and they could rebuild destroyed cities.

CANAAN: "Only in the cities of these peoples that the Lord your God is giving you as an inheritance, you shall not leave alive anything that breathes. But you shall utterly destroy them, the Hittite and the Amorite, the Canaanite and the Perizzite, the Hivite and the Jebusite, as the Lord your God has commanded you, so that they may not teach you to do according to all their detestable things which they have done for their gods, so that you would sin against the Lord your God" (Deut. 20:16-18).

AMALEK: "Now go and strike Amalek and utterly destroy all that he has, and do not spare him; but put to death both man and woman, child and infant, ox and sheep, camel and donkey." (1 Sam. 15:3-4 NAS95)

3. A third level of judgment was for Hazor, Heshbon and Bashan. These cities were all on the borders of biblical Israel. There all people were killed, but animals and valuables were spared.

HAZOR: "All the spoil of these cities and the cattle, the sons of Israel took as their plunder; but they struck every man with the edge of the sword, until they had destroyed them. They left no one who breathed." (Josh. 11:14)

HESHBON: "So we captured all his cities at that time and utterly destroyed the men, women and children of every city. We left no survivor. We took only the animals as our booty and the spoil of the cities which we had captured." (Deut. 2:34-35)

BASHAN: "We utterly destroyed them, as we did to Sihon king of Heshbon, utterly destroying the men, women and children of every city. But all the animals and the spoil of the cities we took as our booty." (Deut. 3:6-7)

4. A fourth level of judgment was for the sub-tribe of Midian, where all the men, women and boys were killed, but girls, animals and valuable objects were spared. Midian was located in the Arabian peninsula, even further from Israel than Hazor, Heshbon and Bashan.

"So they made war against Midian, just as the Lord had commanded Moses, and they killed every male….And Moses said to them, "Have you spared all the women? "Behold, these caused the sons of Israel, through the counsel of Balaam, to trespass against the Lord in the matter of Peor, so the plague was among the congregation of the Lord. Now therefore, kill every male among the little ones, and kill every woman who has known man intimately. But all the girls who have not known man intimately, spare for yourselves" (Num. 31:7, 15-18).

The judgment against Midian is unusual, in that it ordered the death of the adult women but not the girls, as mentioned in the previous chapter. The Bible says in this case the grown women were specifically implicated in the plot to destroy Israel. The young girls were too young to be part of this, and so were spared.

5. A fifth level of judgment was for cities well outside Canaan that fought against Israel: Women, children, animals and valuables were spared.

"When you approach a city to fight against it, ... if it ... makes war against you, ... you shall strike all the men in it with the edge of the sword. Only the women and the children and the animals and all that is in the city, all its spoil, you shall take as booty for yourself. ... Thus you shall do to all the cities that are very far from you, which are not of the cities of these nations nearby" (Deut. 20:10-15).

6. The least restrictive judgment of all was for cities far from Israel which surrendered. They only had to provide labor and tribute to the Israeli government.

"When you approach a city to fight against it, you shall offer it terms of peace. If it agrees to make peace with you and opens to you, then all the people who are found in it shall become your forced labor and shall serve you" (Deut. 20:10-15).

We may not understand all that God did in these judgments, but it is clear that they were not arbitrary and they were proportional.

Also, God does not have a double standard, as he applies the same judgment to Israel, his own people. In Deut. 13:12-18 the Lord says that any Israeli town that turns from the truth to idols should be destroyed, people and animals killed, and that it should never be rebuilt. This is the most severe judgment (the same as used against Jericho) but here it applies to God's own people. God plays no favorites.[42]

---

42   Deut. 13:12-18 NASB: "If you hear it said about one of the towns the Lord your God is giving you to live in that troublemakers have arisen among you and have led the people of their town astray, saying, 'Let us go and worship other gods' (gods you have not known), then you must inquire, probe and investigate it thoroughly. And if it is true and it has been proved that this detestable thing has been done among you, you must certainly put to the sword all who live in that town. You must destroy it completely, both its people and its livestock. You are to gather all the plunder of the town into the middle of the public square and completely burn the town and all its plunder as a whole burnt offering to the Lord your God. That town is to remain a ruin forever, never to be rebuilt, and none of the condemned things are to be found in your hands. Then the Lord will turn from his fierce anger, will show you mercy, and will have compassion on you. He will increase your numbers, as he promised on oath to your ancestors—because you obey the Lord your God by keeping all his commands that I am giving you today and doing what is right in his eyes."

13. Delegation

Few condemn God for ruling over his own creation. After all, he is God. He made us, and he has the right to judge us. God will judge everyone in the world when Christ returns. He has already judged Sodom and Gomorrah, and destroyed those cities himself. He did not ask anyone to do that for him. He did the same to the people before the flood. He was the one who sent the floodwaters and the rain. No man was involved.

But with Canaan, Midian, Amalek and the surrounding areas, he told the Jewish people to execute his judgments. Why did he not just wipe out these people himself? Why did he ask his chosen people to do it?

This is the hard part of the story.

So, the question is, does God have the right to delegate his judgments to men?

Looking at the Bible we see he has done that already in many cases. He has delegated his authority to human judges. He leaves to us the execution of those judgments:

"You shall appoint for yourself judges and officers in all your towns which the Lord your God is giving you, according to your tribes, and they shall judge the people with righteous judgment." (Deut. 16:18) These judges had the right and responsibility to condemn to death:

"The man who acts presumptuously by not listening to the priest who stands there to serve the Lord your God, nor to the judge, that man shall die; thus you shall purge the evil from Israel" (Deut. 17:12).

Similarly the New Testament says that governmental authorities are established by God to punish evil and to put evildoers to death:

"Every person is to be in subjection to the governing authorities. For there is no authority except from God, and those which exist are established by God....for it is a minister of God to you for good. But if you do what is evil, be afraid; for it does not bear the sword for nothing; for it is a minister of God, an avenger who brings wrath on the one who practices evil." (Rom. 13:1-4).

We do not doubt God's right to take someone's life, although we may question his timing. He is God and we are not. Floods, earthquakes, diseases all take lives every day. Little children, women and the elderly die. You will die. I will die. Sometimes these are even called acts of God by the insurance industry.

But as seen, God also delegates to people the right to judge and rule. The Bible even says that Christians will help God judge people at the end of the world.

"Do you not know that the saints will judge the world? If the world is judged by you, are you not competent to constitute the smallest law courts? Do you not know that we will judge angels? How much more matters of this life?" (1 Cor. 6:2-3). In this respect, when the Jews carried out God's judgments against Canaan, it foreshadowed the end of the

world when Christians will rule with Christ: "He who over-
comes, and he who keeps My deeds until the end, to him I
will give authority over the nations, and he shall rule them
with a rod of iron…" (Rev. 2:26-27). So this order to his
chosen people to execute his judgment against the Canaanites is in keeping with God's delegation of judicial authority
to his people. It is, just the same, very hard for us to understand God's sweeping judgment against the Canaanites.

But in our struggle with this issue, as previously noted,
we need to remember:

• It was based on the evil in those societies.

• It was proportional — the more corrupt the region, the
more severe the punishment.

• Many of those who died, such as children, went to
heaven.

• It was protective, as God's intent in all of this was to
save mankind through the coming of the Messiah, who had
to be born in Israel of a Jewish mother.

Theologian Bill Arnold reiterates this:

"There are two reasons for this total destruction…. The
unstated reason is that the Israelites were instruments of
God's judgment; the conquest was not only the means by
which God granted his people the promised land, but was
also the means by which he executed his judgment on the
Canaanites for their sinfulness (see Deut. 9:4). The second
reason ... appears in Deut. 20:18; if the Canaanites survived,
their unholy religion could turn Israel aside from serving the
Lord." [43]

Similarly, Chuck Smith, founder of the Calvary Chapel

43   Arnold, Bill. *The New International Commentary on the Old Testament* (Deut. 20:16)
Eerdman's Publishing, Grand Rapids MI. ISBN: 978-0-8028-2170-6

denomination, writes: "It would be much like you being a guard at a school watching over the kindergartners, ... observing a little dog running up the street with foam coming out of his mouth yipping and nipping at everything. And you immediately recognize the symptoms. ... You know that it has hydrophobia, rabies. Now, would you be justified in killing that little rabid dog before it could get on the school grounds? ... In fact, you would be at fault if you didn't kill that rabid dog. ... You would be responsible for the children's death. ... Now, these people were like rabid dogs ... So God was seeking to protect his innocent children from these destructive practices of these people, and thus He ordered their eradications. Where the nations weren't involved so deeply, God didn't order that kind of eradication." [44]

14. Other explanations

There are many responses to the questions about the violence in the Bible. These can be grouped in five categories.

1) Most Christians believe God is good, the Bible is true, and there are explanations for these passages. This is the approach of this book.

2) Others say that the Bible has been misinterpreted and it is actually not calling for the deaths of the Canaanites, as noted by theologian C. S. Cowles. [45]

3) Some say that these parts of the Bible are not inspired by God, or are just the writings of a violent people in a barbaric time. This is similar to the approach taken by Marcion (c. A.D. 80-160) and contemporary author Eric Seibert.[46]

4) Some say that it is a mystery, or offer no specific answer, saying we should trust God. Theologian L. Daniel Hawk writes against "debates about the rightness or wrongness of interpretations [of biblical violence]" saying they contribute to divisions among Christians.[47]

5) Lastly, some, like atheist Richard Dawkins, take these

---

45   Cowles, C.S., "The Case for Radical Discontinuit," from *Show Them No Mercy,* Gundy, Stanley N. series editor. Zondervan, 2003.
46   Seibert, Eric. *Disturbing Divine Behavior* (Fortress Press, 2009).
47   Hawk, L. Daniel, *The Violence of the Biblical God,* (Grand Rapids, Wm. B. Eerdmans Publishing Co., 2019), p. 203.

passages to mean that Christianity is violent and should be rejected as false, or that God does not exist at all.

* * *

There are problems, in my opinion, with each of these last four approaches. Let us take them one at a time.

2: MISINTERPRETED: I think this one is the most easily disproved. There are too many passages about God's judgment in the flood, Sodom and Gomorrah, Amalek, etc., to think they could have been misinterpreted. The passages are clear. If it was a case of a possible mistranslation of one word or two, then this approach might work. But the clarity, consistency and quantity of these passages do not allow that. That is why they are troubling to many.

3: UNINSPIRED: Those who say these passages are not from God create more problems than they solve. First of all, the passages all make it clear that it is God who ordered these judgments. So if we accept that these are uninspired parts of the Bible, then the Bible is lying when it says that God ordered these judgments. At that point we have to ask, if these passages are false, then what other biblical passages are false? Is the Bible also wrong when it says Christ was raised from the dead? Is heaven real? If God could not protect his own word from lies, then what does that say about God?

4) MYSTERY: In my opinion it is not necessary to shrug our shoulders and say these passages are a mystery. There are sufficient explanations, as noted in this book.

Further, by having no explanation we leave the door

open to those who would criticize the Bible and Christianity as barbaric and false.

5) GOD IS A MONSTER OR DOES NOT EXIST. To accept this conclusion is to disregard the scientific, archaeological, historical and prophetic proofs of Christianity. It is to disregard all the evidence in this book that these actions of God were justified. In my opinion, those who choose this option do so because they want this conclusion (that there is no God). They are willing to overlook the facts to arrive at that conclusion.

* * *

No matter which approach is taken, the issue of divine violence is problematic. Some may not like the explanations in this book. Many get hung up on this one subject. They cannot get past it. They must understand it, or in their view, Christianity is false.

I think that is a dangerous approach.

It is like a man sweating inside a very hot house. To cool down all he has to do is turn on his air conditioner. But he doesn't do it. Why? Because he can't believe that little machine can pull cold air out of hot. How can that be? It makes no sense. So he roasts because he does not understand the principles of phase conversion and refrigeration. He is hung up on this issue.

I encourage you to not get hung up on the issue of violence in the Bible. The explanations are there, but if they are hard to understand, then perhaps you can lean on the preponderance of the evidence (see the last chapter) and just simply trust God for an answer. You just don't know what it is yet.

15. God's explanation

There have been many many books and articles written about the violence of God. Many great minds have struggled to understand it, and today more and more people accuse God of evil. Some are deconstructing their faith in God, and this question plays a prominent role in the shipwreck.

But in any court proceeding, the accused has the right to answer the charges against him. So, does God have an answer? Yes.

In fact, he explains himself in every case. It is not a mystery. So let us let him speak for himself.

Regarding killing almost everyone in the flood, as already mentioned, the Bible says God "saw that the wickedness of man was great on the earth, and that every intent of the thoughts of his heart was only evil continually. The Lord was sorry that He had made man on the earth, and He was grieved in His heart." (Gen. 6:5-6)

The whole world had become evil, violent, deeply involved with the demonic, or simply disobedient to God's call, except for Noah's family. No mystery here. God had a reason.

74

For the extermination of everyone in Sodom and Gomorrah, except for Lot and his two daughters, God's word says:

"The men of Sodom were wicked exceedingly and sinners against the Lord" (Gen. 13:13). It says there was a great outcry to God against these cities and "their sin is exceedingly grave." And yet even then God promised not to destroy the cities if he could find just 10 good people in them (Gen. 18:32). But there were not even that many. As a last show of mercy, God sent two handsome angels to the city as a test (Gen. 18:21), but in response the men of the city tried to rape them.

What would you think of a city where just entering it would result in you being raped?

Seems like the Lord had a reason.

The Lord also explained his judgment against the Amalekites and the Midianites. Both of these tribes tried to destroy Israel, through whom God had promised to send a Messiah to save us. As such their attack was not just against the people of God, but against all who would be saved through Jesus.

Amalek tried to destroy Israel through an unprovoked war and Midian tried to destroy Israel through spiritual deception. This led to the deaths of thousands of Israelites. (Num. 31:1-2, 31:16, Num. 25:9). In the case of Midian it is clear that they had demonic counsel via Balaam, and the strategic attack of Amalek on the vulnerable of Israel also implies the same. So the Lord had a reason.

For the Canaanites, God said he ordered their extermination "because of the wickedness of these nations" and to prevent their corruption from affecting Israel (Deut. 9:4, Lev. 18:24-25, Deut. 7:3-4, 20:18). As mentioned earlier, the Canaanites burned their own children alive, had sex with animals and engaged in other perversions.

Sounds like God had reasons.

For the end of the world, when he will put millions to death, God says he will do it because these people will hate and curse God (Rev. 16:9,11, 21), because of their corruption and to repay them for killing the innocent (Rev. 19:2, 16:6).

These people will see God's miraculous power (Rev. 16-9-21) — all the proof anyone could want of God — but instead of repenting, they will hate God and curse him.

The problem is not, therefore, that there are no explanations, but that we don't know them or don't understand them.

But we should not throw the Lord under the bus because of our limited understanding. We need to remember in Rev. 19:1-2, when all will be revealed, that the multitude will cry out "Right and true are your judgments, O God!"

Note that they will NOT cry out, "Cruel and wicked are your judgments, O God!" We will be struck instead by the fairness of all that God has done. We will see and understand then, but right now it is not clear, as it says in 1 Cor. 13:12: "For now we see in a mirror dimly, but then face to face; now I know in part, but then I will know fully just as I also have been fully known."

We understand only partially. It is not clear to us. Because of that, it is dangerous to trust in our limited understanding and condemn God. There are things hidden from us right now, as when the apostle John was told not to write down the words said by the seven thunders (Rev. 10:4), and when Paul the apostle was told not to reveal the things he saw in heaven (2 Cor. 12:4). Secrets will be revealed on the judgment day, and we are told not to judge until then, "when the motives of men's hearts, and the hidden things of darkness will be revealed" (1 Cor. 4:5).

It would be nice if we could understand everything all the time, but the Bible says we know only in part.

What human can say, "I know everything and am qualified to sit in judgment of God!" No one can say that. We do not know everything. And yet we are tempted to condemn God.

Christ on the cross cried out, "My God, my God, why hast thou forsaken me?" He did not know why. Note that at the moment he cried out, nothing happened. The heavens were not rent, time did not stop, no messenger was sent. He got no answer.

And yet he trusted. He weighed the preponderance of the evidence, and he held fast. In trust, he committed his soul to his Father: "'Into your hands I commit my spirit!' And having said this he breathed his last" (Luke 23:46).

If the Lord was right to exterminate the whole world for its wickedness, except for eight people, then he has the same right to exterminate the Amalekites, some of the Canaanites and some of the Midianites.

He will do the same thing at the end of the world. Our creator has every right to do with us as he would. He is a just judge who must punish evil.

How many times do people see pure evil in this world, and cry out to God for justice? They condemn God for doing nothing. And yet when God has eliminated extremely evil societies, we accuse him of cruelty. He is darned if he does, and darned if he doesn't.

The Bible says, regarding God's punishments, that, "It is a terrible thing to fall into the hands of the living God" (Heb. 10:31). Rather than condemn God about things we do not fully understand, we need to be careful.

I do not know if the explanations in this book are sufficient. Perhaps you also are still crying out, "Why?"

May God give you grace to trust him when you do not understand.

We are in a test now, as the next chapter explains. Let us not fail the test.

16. There will be a test

The Bible verses describing the deaths of millions at God's command are not a mistake. I believe they are a test. Some will pass the test, and some won't.

I always hated pop quizzes at school. You had no time to prepare for them. You walked into class, and boom, there was a test. God also gives surprise tests.

For example, he gave one in John 6. It was not announced in advance. It was a pop quiz. Here Jesus is confronted by an unholy and unruly crowd, which is following him only because he had just miraculously provided food. The idea of free food for life really motivated them and so they decided to make him their king, whether he liked it or not.

John 6:15 says, "they were intending to come and take Him by force to make Him king."

They did not care what Jesus wanted, which was to save us from our sins. Jesus had a higher call in mind, but they didn't. So Jesus told them: "The truth of the matter is that you want to be with me because I fed you, not because you believe in me" (John 6:26 TLB). But his rebuke had no effect. So Jesus realized he had to separate himself (and his

KILLER GOD

true followers) from this crowd. They had an entirely different vision for him, and there was no way to mix the two. He
decided to test everyone in order to get rid of the free lunch
crowd. Since food was their prime motivator, Jesus devel-
oped a test that went directly at that: he put his own flesh on
the menu.

Here is what he said: "With all the earnestness I possess
I tell you this: Unless you eat the flesh of the Messiah and
drink his blood, you cannot have eternal life within you. But
anyone who does eat my flesh and drink my blood has eternal life, and I will raise him at the Last Day. For my flesh is
the true food, and my blood is the true drink" (John 6:53-55
TLB).

These words were too much. But in case they were
inclined to ignore them, Jesus repeats this invitation to cannibalism several times. Of course, he was speaking symboli-
cally, of communion, which in itself is a symbol of the sacrifice of his body and blood on the cross to save us. He really
was not suggesting cannibalism.

But the crowd misunderstood. And Jesus knew they
would. He sounded crazy.

John 6:66 says: "As a result of this many of His disciples
withdrew and were not walking with Him anymore." They
failed the test. But his true followers did not.

"Then Jesus turned to the Twelve and asked, 'Are you
going too?' Simon Peter replied, 'Master, to whom shall we
go? You alone have the words that give eternal life" (John
6:68-69).

In the same way, I believe these passages about divine
violence are a test. They are easy to misunderstand. If we are
not careful, we also can fail the test, and walk away.

The apostle Paul warns us against this: "Don't let others spoil your faith and joy with their philosophies, their wrong and shallow answers built on men's thoughts and ideas, instead of on what Christ has said." (Col. 2:8 TLB).

After all is considered, we need to weigh the preponderance of the evidence and make a decision. That is the subject of the last chapter.

17. Preponderance of the evidence

I have often used the illustration of my wife standing me up on a date. (Now, to keep me out of trouble, let me say that she has never done this! This is just an illustration!)

It is a good way to explain the principle of the preponderance of the evidence.

Imagine that my wife was due to meet me on the street corner one evening for a romantic dinner.

I go to the corner at the appointed time, and she does not show. A cold rain is falling, and as I stand there, I get soaked to the skin. I wait half an hour, and she still does not show. I am miserable and upset. So what do I do?

I can get insulted, and call my lawyer and tell him to prepare divorce papers. I can put an end to this relationship. Clearly she does not love me.

Alternatively, I can recall the preponderance of the evidence which is:

1) We have been married 43 years.

2) She has always been honest and loving to me.

3) There may be things I do not know — maybe she had

a flat tire. Maybe she got hurt and is in the hospital. Maybe her cell phone's battery died. There are too many possibilities to name. What IS clear is that based on the preponderance of the evidence, it is way too soon to conclude that my dear wife is evil. It is way too soon to walk away from a relationship of 43 years because of something I do not understand.

I will instead trust that she has a good reason, and I will know it when I see her next.

It is a mistake to assume that men will always understand women, and vice versa. It is also a mistake to assume we will always understand God. The Bible is full of examples of good people who did not understand what God was doing at the time, but they did later.

Abraham did not understand why God gave him no son for so many years, but he trusted anyway until the day he held his son in his arms. Joseph did not understand why he was sold as a slave and falsely imprisoned, but the day came when the dream he had from God came true. He trusted until then.

In the same way, the preponderance of the evidence for God leads me to hold on to him, even if I do not understand all that he does.

As Job said, "Though he slay me, yet will I trust in him" (Job 13:15). Job said this after a lifetime of God's faithfulness to him and after many blessings. He had seen enough of God to know not to doubt him in his dark night of the soul. He held on.

The many cases where we DO understand God—especially regarding the reliability of the Bible and the faithfulness of God—leads us to trust God in the few cases where we do NOT understand. This short book cannot cover all the evidence of God's love for us and the reliability of his word, but I will list some of them:

God's love for us is shown first of all in the cross. God himself died for my sins. He took on himself all of my ugly words, terrible thoughts and hurtful actions. He took my garbage, and gave me his purity. He was humiliated and beaten for me. He gave up all for me, and for you, even his own Son.

"God demonstrates His own love toward us, in that while we were yet sinners, Christ died for us" (Rom. 5:8).

We cannot concentrate on God's judgments and ignore his love. To reach the right conclusion, we need to see the whole picture.

The fact that God exists is proven. Studies show that most people in the world believe in God. They have differences on God's nature, but they believe. Only 13 percent of the world defines itself as atheist. And as previously mentioned, most atheists believe in the supernatural world. [48]

Why such a widespread belief in God? Because God has put within each of us the knowledge of his existence. Ps. 19 says there is no place in the world where this knowledge has not gone. The Bible says we are all without excuse, because "what can be known about God is plain to them, because God has shown it to them" (Rom. 1:19-20).

We all pray when we are in trouble, even atheists. I once was mocked by a Russian army officer for believing in God. I then asked him, since he was a soldier, if he had ever been in such a dangerous situation that he had prayed. He admit-

---

48   https://web.archive.org/web/20121016062403/http://redcresearch.ie/wp-content/uploads/2012/08/RED-C-press-release-Religion-and-Atheism-25-7-12.pdf, accessed Dec. 16, 2022

ted he had prayed, and we both laughed. There are no atheists in foxholes. Everyone, down deep, believes.

Besides putting in each of us this truth ("God has given to each man a measure of faith," Rom. 12:3), he has surrounded us with the beauty of his creation, a beauty that takes our breath away. There can be no creation without a creator. Something does not come from nothing. The Big Bang theory is accepted by scientists worldwide, and it says the universe had a beginning and will have an end, just like the Bible says.

He who is love shows us love through our spouses, our children and others. He teaches us about his love for us, by letting us experience love. God daily provides for us, sending his rain on the good and the bad.

His desire is to be with us, to walk in the garden with us as he did Adam and Eve, because he loves us. We want to be with those we love.

We have a huge weight of evidence for God's truth. The Bible has been proven precisely correct by archaeology, by history, by science and by fulfilled Biblical prophecies. Most of all God reveals himself in Jesus. There has never been anyone like him. The world dates itself by the birth of Jesus of Nazareth.

Millions of transformed lives prove that God is good and that he is alive. The preponderance of the evidence is all around us.

That is why we should trust God in regard to his judgments in the past and in the future. I believe he has a good reason, and I will know it when I see him next.

BIBLIOGRAPHY

Dawkins, Richard. *The God Delusion.* New York: Mariner, 2008.

Gundry, Stanley N. *Show Them No Mercy: 4 Views on God and Canaanite Genocide.* Zondervan, 2003.

Hawk, L. Daniel. *The Violence of the Biblical God,* Grand Rapids: Wm. B. Eerdmans Publishing, 2019.

Lamb, David T. *God Behaving Badly: Is the God of the Old Testament Angry, Sexist and Racist?* InterVarsity Press, Downers Grove IL, 2011

McDowell, Josh. *The New Evidence that Demands a Verdict.* Nashville: Thomas Nelson Publishers, 1999.

Seibert, Eric A. *Disturbing Divine Behavior: Troubling Old Testament Images of God.* Minneapolis: Fortress, 2009.

Trimm, Charlie. *The Destruction of the Canaanites.* Grand Rapids: Wm. B. Eerdmann's Publishing. 2022.

Whitcomb, John C, and Morris, Henry M. *The Genesis Flood.* Grand Rapids: Baker Book House, 1961.

Wright, Christopher J.H. *Old Testament Ethics for the People of God.* Downers Grove: InterVarsity Press. 2004